# Methods for Leaving a Trace

# Methods for Leaving a Trace

# Table Of Contents

# Introduction



*Legacies aren't automatic; they are carefully built.*

*You have to cherish the right goals and ideals.*

*This eBook tells you how you should go about it.*

# Chapter 1:

How to Leave a Legacy

# Summary

*Leaving a legacy is something most people don't consciously think about, and those that do, are thinking of a larger picture, something that's bigger than life itself. But, how do you leave a legacy for others to follow and peruse?*

# How to Leave a Legacy

Does the thought of leaving behind a legacy make you feel very small? Oh no, this is not for me, I am not Abraham Lincoln or Albert Einstein or Mother Theresa! Think again. For a change, don't think of such great internationally acclaimed icons of achievement. Think of someone around you – your friend or relative or colleague at the office or your priest, just anyone who is or was a part of your daily life.

What do you instantly remember about him or her? Did he do something good for you or others? Did she create something special that benefitted other people? Did they fight some small injustice in the system and change the rules for better? So you recall that stern old Murphy, your manager at the factory was also a kind and fair boss who was loved and respected by all your co-workers. It strikes you that it was your uncle Jim who led tithe fight to save the old Art Deco cinema house on your street from the wrecking ball and got it registered as a heritage property. And your mother's incredible apple pies are spoken of by every family for three blocks down the road, all because she generously shared her recipe and egged on the young housewives till they perfected the Art of the Apple Pie!

There you are...that is legacy! When individuals imprint their deeds in the hearts and mind of people around them, they leave behind a legacy. Now think...what do people recall when they think of you right now? Good stuff? Bad stuff? Sad stuff? Oh, you never gave it a thought, did you? Maybe folks around you don't recall you at all...

Uh oh, that probably makes you feel even smaller than before. But you now know what it means to leave a legacy, and how even the humblest person can leave behind a legacy. So get cracking, bang into the game and start doing YOUR thing – those simple but amazing deeds that will leave behind YOUR legacy.

# Chapter 2:

Be a Famous Grandfather (Or Grandmother)

# Summary


*Beginning small is the right way to begin.*

# Be a Famous Grandfather (Or Grandmother)

You have just celebrated your sixtieth birthday and you are feeling as rotten as hell. Why? Because you suddenly realize that you are not going to leave anything valuable or tangible behind. Yes, you know you have been a good son, husband and father, but what about those great legendary stories that are told about certain persons? Will anyone talk about you in proud awe of something great that you did? Are you leaving behind a legacy?

I'm already an old grandfather, you think, what can I do now? Isn't it too late? Come again, you said you are a grandfather, did you? That itself is a much powerful asset.

Have you noticed that many friends around you always talk about their grandparents? Not that their grandmother or grandfather built the Statue of Liberty or something, but just simple things. They talk about when Grandpop took them fishing down at the river and the great time they had. Or the fact that in the bad old days, Grandmother took the pains to collect scraps of cloth from the local tailor and stitched new trousers for them kids!

Are you spending any such quality time with your grandchildren? Are you going on adventures with them, or giving them good advice? Something that they will talk about in hushed tones when remembering their childhood? A daughter pays tribute to the grandfather of her sons in the poem below:-

> *"He loved everyone that's here, and some he never met,*
> *a man of patience and kindness, I know we won't forget.*
> *My boys loved him dear, with just a bushel and a peck,*
> *and never could they leave without a hug around the neck."*
>
> *-Mynda Res*
>
> *(http://www.familyfriendpoems.com/family/poetry.asp?poem=2425)*

You have a vast repertoire of your life experiences that you can share with your grandchildren. You can impart your work skills and your life skills to them, a little every day. They will learn from your mistakes and be inspired by your success and someday they will say – 'You know, my grandfather used to say..." That's when you will know deep in your spirit, that you have become a 'famous grandfather' and have left behind a great legacy.

# Chapter 3:

Taking Charge of Time

# Summary

*People who leave rich legacies behind are aware of the importance of the richest asset of all – time.*

# Taking Charge of Time

One of the great motivational speakers of this century Rev Billy Graham says – *'The legacy we leave is not just in our possessions, but in the quality of our lives. …The greatest waste in all of our earth, which cannot be recycled or reclaimed, is our waste of the time that God has given us each day.'*

In the words of an anonymous sage –

> *"This is the beginning of a new day.*
> *You have been given this day to use as you will.*
> *You can waste it or use it for good.*
> *What you do today is important*
> *Because you are exchanging a day of your life for it.*
> *When tomorrow comes, this day will be gone forever;*
> *In its place is something that you have left behind...*
> *Let it be something good."*

You have always been concerned about getting value for your money when you go shopping. But are you getting value for the time in your life? Are the hours being squandered away in front of the idiot box? Are days passing away pointlessly? Can you remember what you did three days back?

If you cannot, then you are throwing away the most precious resource of your life. Time is the most important building block of your legacy. Someday you may have a lot of money and people working for you, but you will have run out of time. You can't borrow time. No one will lend it to you.

So the moment to start working on your legacy is NOW.

Get off that couch and do one small thing that will stand for you – write a page of prose, reach out to a needy neighbor, send a letter to your local paper about an issue that troubles you, teach the local kids how to play the saxophone, organize a community cleanup, invent a better drinking straw, shoot a video and upload it on YouTube...

You are the boss. You call the shots. For every day of your life, demand that you get your fair share of life and its rewards. Give notice that henceforth you have Taken Charge of Your Time!

# Chapter 4:

A Sense of Meaning and Purpose

# Summary

*You must know why you exist. There is some reason for you being here.*

# A Sense of Meaning and Purpose

You have everything you need-a nice house, good food, a loving family, a great job atmosphere and good friends. But still a nagging emptiness haunts your life. Clouds of depression still trouble your perfect life. What on earth could be missing from your life?

Stephen R. Covey, one of the most successful New Age gurus completes the picture in this great quote –

*"There are certain things that are fundamental to human fulfillment. The essence of these needs is captured in the phrase 'to live, to love, to learn, to leave a legacy'. The need to live is our physical need for such things as food, clothing, shelter, economical-well being, and health. The need to love is our social need to relate to other people, to belong, to love and to be loved. The need to learn is our mental need to develop and to grow. And the need to leave a legacy is our spiritual need to have a sense of meaning, purpose, personal congruence and contribution in our life."*

You may notice that the first three needs of Live, Love and Learn are qualities we share to some extent with all animal life on earth. But the fourth quality is uniquely human. Only Man wishes to do something great in his lifetime, something that he or she can leave as a legacy. Only Man seeks a 'sense of meaning' in his life. Only Man asks – why am I here? How will I be remembered when I am gone?

One of the greatest benefits you will gain from working consciously and deliberately on your legacy is a sense of meaning and purpose in your life. This brilliant uplifting feeling will quickly sweep away any depressing thoughts of low self esteem. You will be buoyed up by your own deeds and thoughts as you work steadily toward a tangible achievement every day. Throw away your Prozac, the euphoria of living a Legacy is here!

# Chapter 5:

Go Viral!

# Summary

*Nothing works like a little viral publicity.*

# Go Viral!

It has been said, if you want to leave a legacy that lasts for a long time, you should write a bestseller book or compose a hit song or build a great structure. In the past, creating such a work took a long time. More time would pass before a book or poem or song or film spread to the rest of the world and received the critical recognition you have been hoping for.

But in today's world, one does not have to wait for ages to sell a million copies or wait for peer recognition. We are in the era of digital video, Internet and YouTube! We have vast resources at our fingertips with Google, Bing and Wikipedia. Gifted individuals like Olav Per Kindgren and younger personalities like 'Fred Figglehorn' and Natalie Tyler Tran of Community Channel have millions of people enjoying watching their music and videos.

In today's world, if you have something valuable and entertaining to give to the world, a video of your expression can spread virally across the world in days or even hours !

Just imagine you shoot a video on your cell phone, edit it with some online software and upload it on YouTube. It spreads through friends and friends of friends and before you know it, you have created a lasting legacy in the realms of cyberspace. Virtual space it may be, but there are real people watching these videos and gaining and being inspired by them, so such a legacy is also very real and life impacting.

But how can I compete on YouTube with those millions of people uploading everyday? The secret to this unique video that will go viral is YOU again! You are different from all the billions of people on this planet and YOU have something different to say or do. Just think well about what you are good at and start planning a good video today. Get a camera and shoot yourself doing your special thing. And upload. And sit back and watch your own little legacy go viral!

# Chapter 6:

5 Things You Can Do Now for the Hereafter

# Summary

*Start now to be there tomorrow.*

# 5 Things You Can Do Now for the Hereafter

Leaving behind a legacy by the deeds you do in your lifetime is very important. But how you share and transmit your worldly assets after you have passed on can also contribute tremendously to your legacy.

Here are 5 steps you can take to achieve a tangible and lasting legacy through your assets:-

1. Reflect wisely on your priorities and prepare a will. Leave behind a gift or a specific fund for your favorite not-for-profit organization. Ensure that you also name alternate beneficiaries, should those organizations cease to exist.

2. If you have pension plans or life insurance policies in surplus of family needs, bequeath part of that amount to a charity that you are familiar with. Every asset- be it money, real estate, personal belongings and memorabilia should be accounted for in your will.

3. Setup scholarships for needy students or other individuals in niches that may be neglected by State funds. Decide whether you want anonymity or that these pledges should be in your name or the names of your parent or child or any other individual or institution.

4. Encourage friends and family members to contribute to such scholarships and charity funds.

5. Donate your most personal asset - your body – to the State, to enable organ transplants after your demise.

# Chapter 7:

5 Things You Can Do Starting Today

# Summary

*What would you do to build your legacy?*

# 5 Things You Can Do Starting Today

The Egyptians left behind the Great Pyramids as their legacy. Gustave Eiffel is remembered for the Eiffel Tower. Elvis Presley and the Beatles gave us hundreds of hit songs while Bob Dylan continues to add to his already huge legacy! What is your legacy going to be? Here are 5 ideas to get you working on your legacy right away at this very moment:-

→ Write your book. Don't worry about it having to compete with Stephen Covey or Stephen King or any other Stephen! Just let it be about your own experiences and your viewpoint. It can be a novel or a non-fiction book about your area of expertise. Even if you are no expert, go to the library or browse the Net and come up with ideas and information to fill a whole book. Just give all that text your own twist.

→ Build your own house. You were going to build your new house anyway right? Let it be something unique in your neighborhood or even in the state or country or the world! Why settle for a humdrum architectural design? Use your own ideas, use radically different 'green' materials! Let it stand out as your legacy to architecture by reflecting your ideas. Just think outside the masonry box!

→ Teach your children well. As the song by Crosby Stills & Nash goes: "Teach your children well...And feed them on your dreams...The one they picked, the one you'll know by." Invite the kids in your neighborhood and teach them a new skill or coach them at baseball, for free. They will never forget you and who knows, you may just be mentoring the next Babe Ruth or Willie Mays!

→ Invent something. It could be something as simple as a better paper clip or as large as a better Hadron Collider. Apply your mind to a problem and allow your subconscious to pop up a solution. Be sure to apply for a patent, even if it is a simple little invention. Remember Post-Its!

→ Travel the country with a message. Take an important issue, small or large, and take some money and get on the trail. Explain the issue to people and lobby for reform. The media will catch up on you and you will be heard. And you will meet tons of new people and see loads of new places. That little bit of reform will be your legacy.

# Chapter 8:

5 More Things You Can Start Right Away

# Summary


*Here are 5 more things for leaving your legacy that you can start implementing this very moment.*

# 5 More Things You Can Start Right Away

Emperor Shahjehan built the Taj Mahal. Mikhail Gorbachev left behind his legacy of 'glasnost' reform. Jerry Lee Lewis gave us 'Great balls of Fire!' What towering triumph will you leave behind? Relax; it doesn't have to be something as colossal as the Statue of Liberty. Here are 5 simple ways you can work on your own legacy right now:-

→ Institute a Foundation. Use your resources and assets to set up a foundation that will benefit needy people and causes. Prepare a will that assigns funds to non-profit organizations of your choice.

→ Go Viral. Record a song or shoot a video with your cell phone camera and upload it to YouTube. You could even just be expressing your views in a different way that resonates with viewers out there. Before you know it, your clip may go viral and gain thousands and millions of hits, thus getting enshrined in the cyberspace halls of fame.

→ Make lemonade. Not literally of course. When fate hands you a lemon, you must get up and make lemonade! Every adversity holds opportunities for you to create a new legacy. Is your locality struck by a typhoon? Volunteer with the emergency services. Lost a dear one to a dreaded illness? Study and speak out about that disease. Christopher Reeves showed he was a true Superman when he campaigned for better research, even while he was bound in his wheelchair!

→ Heal your family. Every family carries down the burdens of old feuds and attitudes. Trace out all your family members and draw a family tree. Resolve your differences and bring everyone together this Thanksgiving. Your happy great grandchildren will remember your unifying legacy.

→ Gift something unusual. This is something very simple you can do. Instead of the usual knick knacks from the mall, give your friends something different this season. It could be a whole tree planted in their garden, or a photo book with your memories with them or a paid course to study a new language! They will remember you as a friend who was unique and who made a difference in their lives.

# Chapter 9:

Run and Spread the Message

# Summary

*You have to let people know.*

# Run and Spread the Message

Serge Roetheli of Switzerland began his run around the world in 2000 at the age of 47, eventually covering 37 countries in 6 continents. Rosie Swale-Pope of England began running at 57 years of age and covered over 20,000 miles in her run around the world.  Paul Staso, an ultra endurance athlete and founder of PACE Fitness Foundation who has also run across the US says that over 200 people have run across the United States, with a dozen or so actually running solo. What guts!

What is it that makes people run across countries and even the world? In the celebrated film 'Forrest Gump', the main character played by Tom Hanks gets up one morning and starts running, traversing the US 3-4 over five years.

When asked why he ran, Gump says – 'Because I felt like running'. There is something inside us that often makes us want to leave our mediocre lives behind and just run free. And in that free run of our life, we can create a new legacy.

Brian Stark, an English teacher who ran across the country, has this to say – 'I thought my body would be a withering mass after a thousand miles, but it kept getting stronger.'

Many people have coupled their running or travelling across states or countries with a distinct message that they want to spread wherever they go. So you can Run for Peace or 'run to raise funds for cancer research' or 'run for reform'. If physical limitations do not permit you to run, you can drive or simply travel all over, holding meetings or talking to people to spread your unique message.

It is not uncommon to hear of individuals packing some stuff onto a bicycle in India and travelling all over with a simple placard on the bike's front. It is a simple and humble act, but it touches the hearts of people and it brings about change. That simple man on a cycle is creating his own legacy.

# Chapter 10:

Plant Seeds, Many Seeds

# Summary

*It is your seeds that shall eventually bear fruit.*

# Plant Seeds, Many Seeds

18th century America tells us of a man named Johnny Appleseed who went all over the land planting apple seeds. After he had traveled to the end of his journey, he would return along the same path, tending to the little trees that had grown and plating new ones. A vast network of nurseries and grown trees stands today as the legacy of John Chapman, an American pioneer nurseryman, who came to be known as the legendary John Appleseed.

Johnny Appleseed left behind an estate of over 1,200 acres of valuable nurseries, worth millions even then, and far more now. Johnny Appleseed Elementary School now stands in Leominster, Massachusetts, his birthplace.

You can start planting seeds today to institute your own legacy.

You can take this lesson literally and start planting seeds and trees in your neighborhood or all over your state. The environment will be richer for your action and the communities around those trees will naturally benefit from them. If you plant an acorn today, you may not live to see it become a giant oak tree, but your descendants and those who take shelter in the shade of that tree will give thanks to you and your legacy.

Or you can take a metaphorical view and start planting the seeds of education in the garden of young minds. Teach young people whatever you know best – a technical skill, moral lessons, share your life skills. Then nurture them regularly by following up and boosting your students to achieve great ideals. Trim their wayward branches and fertilize their roots with continuing advice.

Every great achiever tells of a mentor, someone who educated and inspired them in their lives and careers. You can be that sage in young people's lives.

And in time you will be known as Timothy Oaktree or Guitar Greg or Vanessa
Vineyard or even Football Fred!

- 43 -

# Conclusion

*It doesn't take genius to leave a legacy behind, but it does ask a lot of other things. By now, you have a clearer picture of what leaving a legacy means.*

*Have fun implementing the methods mentioned in the eBook.*

**All the best to you!!!**